Women Who Don't Blush

by Trishanna Marie

DORRANCE PUBLISHING CO
EST. 1920
PITTSBURGH, PENNSYLVANIA 15238

Dorrance Publishing Co
585 Alpha Drive
Suite 103
Pittsburgh, PA 15238
Visit our website at www.dorrancebookstore.com

ISBN: 979-8-88812-295-2
eISBN: 979-8-88812-795-7

For my incredible daughter, Audrey Jane

THE SCARCITY

ALTERNATIVE SAGE

I christen my apartment walls with the machismo I have collected
Since your embrace became a family of fire ants
And your words became a cold room for my sadness to fog up and draw
faces on
I beg for the day my heart is scooped out
With the cold cream fingertips of
Ryan's and Bryan's and Licky-lipped lions,
Who reach for nipples and nape and thigh
This whole wide world is my sugar cone
Topped off with a syrup of 3am Merlot tears
On Wednesdays my weeping transforms into lubricant for long haired boys
to guzzle
Thursday mornings
Drown ribs
power pressure brain cells
and any memory
Of the doey eyed romantic I used to be
When I saw pink
Now, colorblind
How many times do I have to play black and white Johnny cash songs on repeat?
How many times do I have to gulp down photos and moments and memories
you prostituted?
You turned me into a dollar bill
Even Good ol' Georgey is blushing
You clothed me in scratchy objectification like a mannequin
Now my heart is as plastic as you are
Tell me you love my display
You created it, after all.
Arched heel, vacant eyes

How did I survive this long as a woman?
How are there so many drag queen David's among so many misogynistic Goliaths?
How am I still smiling and nodding to life's nod?
Probably because my bones are made of bruises and my thumbs are frozen on triggered trauma
Dare me to thaw out and pull the fucking trigger
Paralyzed
I keep smiling
Like the men on the streets tell me to do.

COBAIN

He is an old soul
Who adds years to my life
When his smile crinkles to his cheeks
My core is the first time I went too high on a swing
He is the most original person I have ever met and still a novelty
I love to see his soft cotton T whip around ribs
when his board slices through people and places and time
When I give him a hard time or "get on his case," as he would say
I can always tell he's holding back a smile
He secretly loves the untamed in me
It is a warm hug
He kisses like he wants to vacation on my lips
Set up umbrella and sand chair
I drink him in like I want to swallow the ocean and become his antigravity
He does not have to comb his hair or wear fancy jeans
He is organic beauty
I love how he hugs me into a slow dance
And turns my body into his favorite song
He sleeps like he is a different part in a play every night
Monkey. Tin man. Zombie
His eyes are a time lapsed sky
And his hands are clouds that I can always make out to be a bunny or a
dragon or all of me
My cat adores him
We both break down around animals
We turn to mush and comedy
When he cries the mountains and the carpet crumble around me
I yearn to be his fortune cookie
Break me open,

You will find that everything will be okay
When he looks at me
I am Mona Lisa
When I speak I am a novel
He licks his fingers and
flips through tree trunk pages
Never wanting to get to the last
He is not aware of his rarity—
Old man loafers paired with gym shorts
I cannot tell if he is as truly free
As he seems to be
He is multiple ages at the same time
A wild little boy growling and gritting teeth
A teen sneaking tequila
A senior making the bed for me
He is a relevant lover
I hold my breath sometimes
when he puts his hands on the pads of my heels
His skin is salt and milky smooth skipping stones
I beg them to bounce and eventually sink my blue
When he is wrestling my sheets,
resting his head on my shoulder,
and eating up the morning with me
I often imagine the two of us
Untainted by life and society
Color is calm with him
And noise is melody
What would it be
If I was a different person
And so was he?
I, a mother sweeping up wreckage, rebuilding my own captain and ship
Him, a salmon swimming upstream
Pink and powerful

COBAIN REVISED

You are a desert,
the two white webs in the corners of my mouth.
I lick my lips
only to slide the salt of other lovers who have crystalized
on your
sophomoric saliva
They cheapen my rich kiss,
slowly closing in on words and intimacy and right
Little did you know
I am black widow
I take thirsty lacework
and Spiderman shoot your
semen back to you
Even though you have always been
droughty
lushy
fatuous
Open mouthed you beg for my wet
Insatiable and bare footed
You pink your heels
desperate to climb my pyramid
Never, will I allow you to the top
Light your cigarette on heat wave warnings
and keep disintegrating in your broken down
sandy life
Even if my body becomes a well
the moment you turn to dust
Not a raindrop would I offer
unless it meant your copper compliments would rust

JUST A GIRL

I am a gypsy
Your eyes are pockets
filled with all I've robbed
from this world
I am a wave lacking
pure
ivory foam,
lashing at sand selfishly
I am malice disease,
ill derived and washed out
lurking on your final days
I am your tasteless vice—
cigarette filmed cough
pitch lined coffee mugs
repeated whiskey morning breath.
I am an acrobatic enemy
wreaking of abandonment
and contorting demise
I am a mummy
wrapped in lusty linen lies
all the while buried in your arms,
like a pharaoh

I have a gremlin heart
that will gobble up your days
purging a stainless course
I bare a scorpion back
whipping in reverse to pierce your
heated holy heart

My python legs
squeeze your robust piety,
crushing regal goodness.

My wants are bigger than my mouth and tongue and words
And I am just.　　　a.　　　　　girl.

YOU AND I

I am
a soaking secret at best,
Drenched in affliction
I am
a ghost gripping your shadows,
Hunting for the sun
All the while
You are
a voyager
Seeking hands under tables,
Locked doors,
Alleyways,
Elevators,
Vague descriptions and
Protective platonic stances
You are
a true modern-day Columbus,
You find me, a flat dimension of self.
You are
an alluring Copperfield,
Hiding my declarative "no's" under hats
and turning them into whispered "yes's"
Your audience in awe
Unaware of what they are actually applauding

You are
sawed in half
"This can be enough," I tell myself

It isn't.

THE YEARNING

MUSTACHE

My bed is only messed up by me,
Diagonally.
Sleep is an ambush
Soldiers gun at my eyelids
They quiver when natural light
stuffs iris barrels with daisy
If only I could create my own field of weeds
Will man remain my enemy?
I dare a mustache to balk
at my bush
For there is no tongue,
No kiss,
No tooth
In my world
to declare how a woman should be
in her panty
I grip the shadows on my eery layered mattress
held in nuptial tandem
 Right side of the bed or left?
Phantom questions a catalyst for
Moaning opera cries

Ringing and menacing, they haunt me,
Wail to me
 That I am stone
Only the most desolate sleep on me
No stream in the river? A loveless mother?
Go ahead and rest your cheek on my grey

I remain bayside
Crack me open to find lavender clouds
drifting above sweaty skyline
A jagged amethyst,
A gem of a woman
Treated like a skipping stone
That is me
No.
I will become the ocean before that is my identity

MON

Your body is nectar
It shifts and shakes me
Into a yellow and black beauty
I grow wings
But I wouldn't dare to use them
I keep them tucked behind blades
And suck up the honey
That I rinse out of you
I become a fiend
My habit is your hands
I crave
collar bone.
Your pores are pebbles
My ache comes in currents
And soon I am sinking into your soft sands
Your lips are morning dew
That still drip with dusk
I become every hour of the day
I will peer into your motley way
with wreck less abandon
For as long as you will let me.

BURN

A rough surface of sorrow
forms under eyelids
when I see you
Strike it with a match of apathy,
Light your cigarette,
and throw fire to the burn pile of your life.
Flames flicker around
your daughter's botched haircuts
her eyes have the same longing yours do.
Violet heat swirls around questions
trapped in thought bubbles,
they hang over your son's sweet hazel head
His prism tears make
everything go to ash

As I stand an outsider
Poking rod to ember
Even as I prod
I know the only thing I will find
is empty charcoal memories of how we used to be
Before the (w)reckoning

How scorched it feels, how black it hurts
To lose someone who was there through it all
I could always arrive with streaks down my cheeks.
We could always be the kindling.

I guess all I can do now is say
Burn it all down, baby

GRIEF

I lick my wounds with
a sorbet sunset tongue
A slurp so icy thick and orange that it covers elephant horizons
My pain—a mirrored cloud skyscraper
it is king to
Grief
A planet where there are never enough parking spaces
If you find a place to rest
 it will cost you an over-romanticized
sensory memory
You will never sleep again
I expand begging for a white lined fence
Black fills my cracks
my clothes wear me
Everyone tries to hug me
They start their sentences with a dry, choking, "at least."
I start to resent throats
Oxygen is my mother
She shows up
holds my hands tenderly,
rubs fingertips over my nail beds
I beg her to stay
to swaddle and morph me into infancy
She just murmurs, "me too."
"I want that too."
Can I be cotton?
Or the light that fills checkered New York cockroach apartments?
Can I be anything but a woman
grieving over a black shelled conman?

NOVEMBER HELD BY DECEMBER

I only want to write in
the middle of the month
It is safer
hugged between
the beginning
and the
end.
Would January
please help release me
from December's arms?

QUEEN CHEF

With your hands you transform rainbows
that have arched from the earth
You bare down, even in the fervor of summer's firing flame
To consecrate recipes that are born by the grit of the soil, not by nursing
mother
Your loved ones raise hands,
bounce up and down,
begging to be invited around your wooden table
to feast with fierce female culinary queen,
and her well-fed family

THE UPRISING

NARCISSUS

You thumb mute on my mouth

Pushing buttons on all that I share,
You, with silver gun
Staple words on the inside of my molars

Metal bent ends punch through enamel stating:

CRAZY
OVERREACTIVE
BAD MOM
WORTHLESS
FAILURE OF A WIFE
DESERVING OF BEING CHEATED ON

I take tongue and unclip your frantic grasps at control
I push my lips
A dagger through your finger
No longer will you hold me down
The women I came from and the woman I am
Are stronger than any man of your men
Pathetic, you cling to your photographed dick
While I wake up clinging to my core, lovesick

The mask is unveiled
My daughter, so pure
As much as you try you won't turn me frail
I will always endure.
The sun as my witness, my heart rises up in my throat
My truth will never be evoked.

BABY

When she became to be
Within me
She strummed ribs,
Finger picking nylon bones to her fancy
Twirling among a galaxy placenta
I wiggle with her
My fleshy palms press upon apple core
Desperate to know
Was it her elbow or heel or shoulder blade?
A Where's Waldo of baby

The earth found you

I see myself in the way she grips loose hair strands at my nape
her anchor
She holds on the way I have my whole life,
with vigor
she will not be left behind
In a world of brothers

What do I do with all of this life?

PARENT

Pang after pain
My heart sinks to my feet
Every morning
I wake up to maroon socks
A trail of crimson everywhere I step
Reminded
I am not the robins fluttering outside my window
not my cozy cobalt couch,
an abused lover,
not my daughter,
and never YOU.
Freedom will always come with shame
To rest is to sink into blue veins
No one will wipe my nose
Only women will love me like I love her
Like I loved you
I hold onto feminine first aid
like ancient roots into basalt floor

To be the one to crush chested organ with heel
Instead of you.
You suck milky marrow from my bones,
lick your lips on vulnerable aorta
I protect open clavicle with the tentacles of my ancestors,
You fucking vampire
I wipe alligator tears from eyes
My back wrists are sponges,
prepared for this moment.
Every time I breathe, I gulp up salt water

I thrash
Refuse to drown
For her.
You hate that she needs me more
Man of crumbs, I eat you up
Full, I sit without you.

RAISINS

My nipples are
raisins
grape bubble gum faucets
masticated into purple milk
They resurrect into lactose layers,
regurgitated on the scoop of my neck
Where I used to sweep wrists over with Dior's latest—
Now nape exudes hints of expired greek yogurt and sweet snot
Dior Dior,
Someone create a scent that does not
surrender to alcohol
Until I do
Instead of bobbing on land with
lopsided engorged meal tickets
Ankle weighted to an open gummed mouth
I close mine every time anyone asks me how it is to be a mother
Of course, I love her, gaping and all
So unapologetically in want
I envy the way she sprawls open
Screaming and ripping, demanding what she deserves
When is it as women we learn to be hushed, silenced for what we hunger?

PARENTING PLAN

I am a lost and not found item
when she leaves.
I am a scratchy polyester,
Patched elbow sleeve
Left by mustard sidelines,
forgotten when bell rings.
I crumple away in cardboard box,
Puppy eyeing
Any stingy non-owner
Is there a thief to claim me?

My stretched gap knit
is your shallow water
At six foot six
You brag that your toes brush the bottom
of the same dune
That our toddler's touch too

Eventually
her and I will outreign you

All the while the everything of me is
in the deep end,
treading.
I dog paddle to
dolphin attorney
and counselor coy fish
"Help me not drowned?"

I sink and
swallow
Algicide anger
Crunch my lungs on shark teeth
Try to become sacred coral reef
Just for my daughter to find me

AUDREY

Her crumbs cascade waxy floor
I breath
Can I function
intentionally?
My hand rests on chest
I dig fingertips into collarbone
I count
the way I was taught as a child
1… 2… 3
I am still here

Before my daughter sleeps
she begs me to read Mr. & Mrs. Elmo books
I cannot protect her from a fraudulent father and
Imbalanced
teeter totter parenting.
A genetically predisposed man wakes up and occasionally chooses to hold her
I trained my heart to let go of tucked in promises
A LONG TIME AGO
Disneyland Dad strikes again
I hope she views his love like an orange window at sunset
I will not let the line to the ride exist
She will be okay
I echo this
I bite every layer of cheek
Awake and asleep
Her mother is instinct
No choice is involved
I felt her every hiccup

in womb
every twirl and spill and swallow
I beg the orbits of hemisphere
to protect her from her father's contrast
Planted black swimmer
faltered sperm
a fingerprint.
When she opens lids and voice
It is only her
Not her mother
Not her father
She is exquisite.